Contents

WHAT Is a Rube Goldberg Machine?

Rube Goldberg machines—or contraptions—are designed to perform simple tasks in the most complicated, ridiculous, and hilarious way possible. Today, any needlessly complicated machine is called a Rube Goldberg, after its inventor, the cartoonist Reuben Goldberg.

The machines often begin with a simple action that sets off a chain reaction, as shown in these cartoons.

Reuben Lucius Goldberg (1883-1979) was an award-winning political cartoonist. Although Goldberg drew several cartoon series, he became most famous for Professor Lucifer Gorgonzola Butts. Butts was the cartoon inventor of such machines as one that showed how to remove cotton from a bottle of aspirin. Goldberg spent hours designing each machine to make sure that it would actually work. Even though Goldberg drew the zany machines, he never built one.

WHAT'S More . . .

The 1931 Merriam-Webster dictionary included the term "Rube Goldberg" as an adjective. The meaning: "Accomplishing by complex means what seemingly could be done simply."

Reuben Goldberg with his wife and children

TIME FOR KIDS

BOOK OF WHAT

EVERYTHING INVENTIONS

TIME FOR KIDS

Managing Editor, TIME FOR KIDS: Nellie Gonzalez Cutler
Editor, Time Learning Ventures: Jonathan Rosenbloom

Book Packager: R studio T, New York City
Art Direction/Design: Raúl Rodriguez and Rebecca Tachna
Writer: Catherine Nichols
Illustrator: Chris Reed
Photo Researchers: Miriam Budnick, Elizabeth Vezzulla
Designers: Fabian Contreras, Ames Montgomery
Copyeditor: Joe Bomba
Indexer: Charles Karchmer
Fact Checkers: Luis Pereyra, Audrey Whitley

Redesign: Downtown Bookworks, Inc.
Project Manager: Sara DiSalvo

Cover: Symbology Creative

TIME INC. BOOKS

Publisher: Margot Schupf
Vice President, Finance: Vandana Patel
Executive Director, Marketing Services: Carol Pittard
Executive Director, Business Development: Suzanne Albert
Executive Director, Marketing: Susan Hettleman
Publishing Director: Megan Pearlman
Associate Director of Publicity: Courtney Greenhalgh
Assistant General Counsel: Simone Procas
Assistant Director, Special Sales: Ilene Schreider
Assistant Director, Finance: Christine Font
Senior Manager, Sales Marketing: Danielle Costa
Senior Manager, Children's Category Marketing: Amanda Lipnick
Associate Production Manager: Amy Mangus
Associate Prepress Manager: Alex Voznesenskiy
Associate Project Manager: Stephanie Braga

Editorial Director: Stephen Koepp
Art Director: Gary Stewart
Senior Editors: Roe D'Angelo, Alyssa Smith
Managing Editor: Matt DeMazza
Editor, Children's Books: Jonathan White
Copy Chief: Rina Bander
Design Manager: Anne-Michelle Gallero
Assistant Managing Editor: Gina Scauzillo
Editorial Assistant: Courtney Mifsud

Special thanks: Allyson Angle, Keith Aurelio, Katherine Barnet, Brad Beatson, Jeremy Biloon, John Champlin, Ian Chin, Susan Chodakiewicz, Rose Cirrincione, Assu Etsubneh, Mariana Evans, Alison Foster, Kristina Jutzi, David Kahn, Jean Kennedy, Hillary Leary, Samantha Long, Kimberly Marshall, Robert Martells, Nina Mistry, Melissa Presti, Danielle Prielipp, Babette Ross, Dave Rozzelle, Matthew Ryan, Ricardo Santiago, Divyam Shrivastava

Contents of this book previously appeared in TIME FOR KIDS Big Book of WHAT.

For information on TIME FOR KIDS magazine for the classroom or home, go to TIMEFORKIDS.COM or call 800-777-8600. For subscriptions to SI KIDS, go to SIKIDS.COM or call 800-889-6007.

Published by TIME FOR KIDS Books,
An imprint of Time Inc. Books
1271 Avenue of the Americas, 6th floor
New York, NY 10020

ISBN 10: 1-61893-392-2
ISBN 13: 978-1-61893-392-8

TIME FOR KIDS is a trademark of Time Inc.

We welcome your comments and suggestions about TIME FOR KIDS Books. Please write to us at: TIME FOR KIDS Books, Attention: Book Editors, P.O. Box 361095, Des Moines, IA 50336-1095
If you would like to order any of our hardcover Collector's Edition books, please call us at 800-327-6388 (Monday through Friday, 7 a.m.–9 p.m. Central Time).

1 QGT 15

PHOTO CREDITS Cover: Mark Wainwright/Symbology Creative (bkgrnd); LilKar/Shutterstock.com (clouds top); Costazzurra/Shutterstock.com (futuristic car); Iasha/Shutterstock.com (trampoline); Luis Louro/Shutterstock.com (jumping boy); Jorg Hackemann/Shutterstock.com (Zorbing); Chesky/Shutterstock.com (blimp); ©iStockPhoto.com/fotokostic (kevlar vest); ©iStockPhoto/TomasSereda/Thinkstock (clouds bottom); photoart1985/Shutterstock.com (geodesic dome); Stepan Bormotov/Shutterstock.com (boomerang); ©Purstock/Thinkstock (hovercraft). Interior: 1: Mark Wainwright/Symbology Creative (bkgrnd); Djedi Team (Djedi). 2–3: Shutterstock.com/watchara. 3: alvant/Shutterstock.com (camera); NASA (Puffin); Aprilphoto/Shutterstock.com (treasure). 4–5: Color Symphony/Shutterstock.com (bkgrd); Library of Congress, Prints and Photographs Division (Goldberg). 5: Purdue University photo/Vince Walter (winners top left); Purdue University photo/Andrew Hancock (winners bottom left); Purdue University photo/David Umberger (winners right). 6–7: MARGRIT HIRSCH/Shutterstock.com. 6: alvant/Shutterstock.com (camera); Library of Congress, Prints and Photographs Division (portrait). 7: ©Marka/SuperStock (first photograph); ©Science and Society/SuperStock (plaster casts). 8–9: meunierd/Shutterstock.com. 9: Djedi Team (all). 10–11: Horst Kanzek/Shutterstock.com (all). 10: Library of Congress, Prints and Photographs Division. 11: Route66/Shutterstock.com (penny); Hank Frentz/Shutterstock.com (farthing); Public Domain, courtesy of Cornell University (drawing). 12–13: katix/Shutterstock.com (all). 12: Designua/Shutterstock.com. 13: Marcin Balcerzak/Shutterstock.com (hiker); NOAA (geodiesist); Vasileios Karafillidis/Shutterstock.com (stork). 14–15: cozyta/Shutterstock.com. 14: U.S. Pattent & Trademark Office (pattent); Shutterstock.com (braille). 15: Graham Oliver/123RF.com (trampoline); iofoto/Shutterstock.com (earmuffs). 16–17: Laborant/Shutterstock.com. 16: Galushko Sergey/Shutterstock.com (cookies); mffoto/Shutterstock.com (cereal). 17: Africa Studio/Shutterstock.com (chips); Shebeko/Shutterstock.com (ice cream). 18: Serg64/Shutterstock.com (bkgrd); tonyz20/Shutterstock.com (blimp); U.S. Navy (Hindenburg). 19: Mikhail Zahranichny/Shutterstock.com (kevlar vest); TFoxFoto/Shutterstock.com (fireman); Ingi AgnarssonMatjaž KuntnerTodd A. Blackledge/Public Library of Science/Creative Commons (spider webs). 20–21: vic927/Shutterstock.com (bkgrd); David E. Klutho /Sports Illustrated (thrower). 20: Muriel Lasure/Shutterstock.com. 21: Courtesy of Gerhard Walter (all). 22–23: Shutterstock.com. 22: Hulton Archive/Getty Images (Fuller); gattopazzo/Shutterstock.com (diagram). 23: Katherine Welles/Shutterstock.com (Biosphere); Steve Kingsman/123RF.com (Spaceship Earth). 24–25: Vladislav Gajic/Shutterstock.com. 24: The National Archives. 25: ian woolcock/Shutterstock.com (coming ashore); Sgt Richard Blumenstein/United States Marine Corps (on water). 26–27: Serg64/Shutterstock.com (bkgrd); Jorg Hackemann/Shutterstock.com (kids zorbing). 27: Chris Turner/Shutterstock.com (zorbing track); Sergey Lavrentev/Shutterstock.com (water zorbing). 28–29: Toria/Shutterstock.com (bkgrd); ssuaphotos/Shutterstock.com (train). 29: Bob Carey for Segway Inc.. 30–31: watchara/Shutterstock.com. 30: NASA. 31: NASA (International Space Station); leonello calvetti/Shutterstock.com (Earth). 32–33: Aleksandr Bryliaev/Shutterstock.com. 32: Dudarev Mikhail/Shutterstock.com (cow); maxicam/Shutterstock.com (robot). 33: DenisNata/Shutterstock.com (beakers); Volosina/Shutterstock.com (meat); V_ace/Shutterstock.com (hydroponic farm). 34–35: Shutterstock.com. 34: amskad/Shutterstock.com (leatherback turtle); Spotlite Photography/Shutterstock.com (Sumatran oranguatan); Attila JANDI/123RF.com (mountain gorilla); Ugo Montaldo/Shutterstock.com (Atlantic bluefin tuna); ©Juniors/SuperStock (vaquita). 35: ehtesham/Shutterstock.com (tiger); KMW Photography/Shutterstock.com (snow leopard); Chatchai Somwat/123RF.com (Irrawaddy dolphin); ©Mihaic/Dreamstime.com (Javan rhino); tristan tan/Shutterstock.com (Asian elephant). 36–37: Shutterstock.com. 36: Library of Congress, Prints and Photographs Division (settlement); Internet Archive Book Image/Public Domain (Croatoan). 37: American Spirit/Shutterstock.com (memorial); NPS Photo (archaeologists). 38–39: Serg64/Shutterstock.com (bkgrd); National Archives/U.S. Air Force (Earhart); Christos Georghiou/Shutterstock.com (map). 39: National Archives/U.S. Navy. 40–41: Pi-Lens/Shutterstock.com (bkgrd); Aprilphoto/Shutterstock.com (treasure). 40: bahareh khalili naftchali/Shutterstock.com (map); Courtesy of www.oakislandtreasure.co.uk (workers). 41: Courtesy of www.oakislandtreasure.co.uk (all). 42: Library of Congress, Prints and Photographs Division (bkgrd); ©Winchester Mystery House (door, no ceiling). 43: ©Alysonbee/Dreamstime.com (bkgrd); ©Science and Society/SuperStock (Elsie, Frances). 44–45: Pi-Lens/Shutterstock.com (bkgrd); LMPhoto/Shutterstock.com (cave). 45: Marcus Bay/Shutterstock.com (underwater); salajean/Shutterstock.com (man in cave). 46–48: Shutterstock.com/watchara.

Inventions change the way we live. It's hard to imagine our world without earmuffs or the ice-cream cone. In this chapter, you'll discover the amazing stories behind these inventions—and more!

How Zany Can You Get?

Many schools hold contests for students who want to design Rube Goldberg machines. One of the best known is a national event for college students, originally held at Purdue University, in Indiana. All contestants are assigned a specific task, such as "Sharpen a Pencil," "Shut Off an Alarm Clock," or "Zip a Zipper." Each machine is judged on how it performs, the number of steps needed to complete the task, and how well it keeps to the spirit of a Rube Goldberg machine.

Past winners from the National Rube Goldberg competition

WHAT Is a Daguerreotype?

Silver-plated sheets

Click! Today, a digital camera can capture a scene in less than a second. That was not always so. In the early days of photography, it took up to 20 minutes to take a picture. These early photographs, called daguerreotypes (dah-*gehr*-oh-types), were produced by a process developed by Louis Daguerre who lived in France.

To take a daguerreotype, a photographer placed a silver-plated copper sheet covered with iodine into a camera and exposed it to light. Because the material wasn't very sensitive to light, it had to be exposed for a long time. Then the photographer placed the sheet in a cabinet with mercury vapor to develop the image. The fumes from the vapor combined with the silver to produce an image. To stop the developing process, the photographer rinsed the sheet in a salty solution.

Daguerreotypes caught on as more and more people wanted their picture taken. For the first time in history, people could preserve actual images of themselves and their loved ones. Unfortunately, daguerreotypes were very delicate and many of these early photographs faded or fell apart over time. By the 1850s, the daguerreotype became less popular as faster and cheaper ways to take photos became available.

Lens

Camera

WHAT'S More...

Posing for a daguerreotype portrait was time consuming. The process could take as long as 20 minutes. In order to not blur the photo, the person posing couldn't move.

In 1826, Joseph Niepce, a Frenchman who worked with Daguerre, took the world's first photograph. The photo needed an exposure time of eight hours. It shows the view of a city from a window.

The first photograph taken by Daguerre, in 1837, shows plaster casts next to a window.

WHAT Is Djedi?

For hundreds of years, explorers have searched for secret passageways and concealed rooms inside the Great Pyramid of Giza, in Egypt. Now, a robot is finding what no explorer could. The robot, called Djedi, is part of a project led by an international team of researchers.

One of the pyramid's mysteries is what lies in the passageways beyond two eight-inch-square shafts. Because the narrow tunnels climb so high—they are equal to a 13-story building—only a robot can explore the entire length of the tunnel.

In 1993, a different robot reached the end of one of the passageways. But when it drilled through a wall, its camera revealed another wall. Djedi's advanced tools give it greater access, allowing it to explore further.

New Clues to Decode

One of the new robot's features is a snakelike camera, able to fit through small spaces and bend around corners. When Djedi got to the end of a passageway, it pushed its camera through a hole and peeked around the corner. There, it found red hieroglyphs and lines in the stone. The markings were last seen when the pyramid was built, more than 4,500 years ago.

Researchers believe that if the hieroglyphs can be deciphered, they may explain why the tunnels were built. What other secrets are hiding beyond a long shaft or behind a stone door? Perhaps a small robot will reveal the answers.

The Great Pyramid at Giza is the largest of Egypt's 70 pyramids. When it was built, around 2550 B.C., it was about 480 feet high.

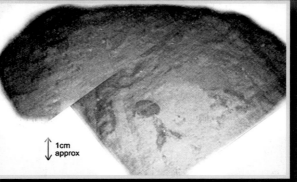

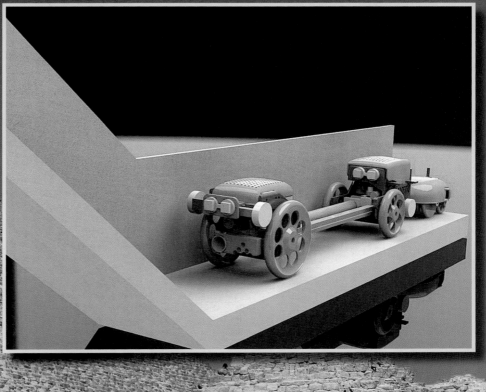

The Djedi robot, below, has been exploring the Great Pyramid. The robot found the red markings at left. What do they mean?

1cm approx

WHAT Is a Penny Farthing Bicycle?

The old-fashioned penny farthing bicycle isn't seen much today, but during the 1870s and 1880s it was a common sight on cobblestone streets. With its extra-large front wheel, tiny back wheel, and tall seat, the penny farthing wasn't the easiest bike to ride. A rider needed a special mount just to climb onto the seat. Stopping the bike was also difficult because a rider couldn't put his foot on the ground. More importantly, the bike's high center of gravity made the bike unstable. Any obstacle, no matter how small, might tip the bike and send its rider flying.

This risk, however, didn't stop the penny farthing from becoming popular. That's because, unlike previous riding contraptions whose wheels were made of wood, the penny farthing had rubber tires, which gave people a much smoother ride. The large front wheel was directly connected to the pedals, which allowed a rider to go faster than ever before.

WHAT'S More...

How did the penny farthing bike get its name? In England, a farthing is a small coin, especially when compared to the much larger English penny. When the two coins are placed side-by-side, they look like the wheels of the high-wheeler bike.

Pedaling the Globe

The first person to circle the world by bike rode a penny farthing. Thomas Stevens set off from San Francisco on April 22, 1884. In his handlebar bag were clothes, a pistol, and a raincoat that doubled as his tent. Stevens rode across the United States along wagon trails, rail tracks, and paved roads. In some areas, he took trains.

When Stevens reached Boston, he sailed to Europe, where he resumed riding. He traveled through the continent to Asia.

Stevens' bike-riding journey ended on December 17, 1886, in Japan. From there he took a ship back to San Francisco. All together he had pedaled 13,500 miles. Stevens later wrote a book about his adventures, titled *Around the World on a Bicycle*.

WHAT Is GPS?

Before maps or compasses were invented, people used the sun and stars to navigate. In a way, we're still looking to the sky when we travel—only now we're looking to high-tech satellites, called the Global Positioning System (GPS).

GPS is a system of satellites, monitoring stations, and receivers. The 28 solar-powered satellites are spaced evenly around Earth and orbit our planet twice a day. Each satellite carries four atomic clocks that send the exact time to receivers on Earth. Each satellite also sends signals that tell its current location. A GPS receiver uses the information to calculate its own position on Earth.

Monitoring Stations

With so many satellites in orbit, it's important to know where each one is located to make sure none stray off course. Monitoring stations set up around the world do just that. The tracking information that the stations receive is relayed to the Master Control Station located at Schriever Air Force Base in Colorado.

Satellites in space send signals to monitoring stations on Earth.

WHAT'S More ...

The United States developed GPS technology for military use. The public was allowed to use the system in 1983, although at first the information wasn't as precise as the military's.

Where Am I?

GPS has many uses on land, sea, and in the air. Besides helping drivers and pilots find their way, GPS keeps hikers on the right trail, and helps fishermen locate where the fish are biting. Golfers use it to measure the distance between holes.

Scientists use GPS to help them with their research, such as studying earthquake faults or discovering the migration patterns of animals. Explorers hunting for shipwrecks guide their vessels with GPS. And, perhaps most importantly, emergency teams responding to disasters use GPS to locate victims.

A hiker uses GPS to plan his route through the woods.

By using GPS, a geodesist (a scientist who specializes in the measurement of the earth) can monitor the movement of a site 24 hours a day, seven days a week.

A scientist attaches a GPS device to a stork, to gain information about its navigation.

WHAT Are Some Inventions by Kids?

Inventors are a curious bunch, and many started tinkering and experimenting when they were kids. Here's a look at four inventions still in use today. What do they have in common? All were thought up by young inventors!

WHO Margaret Knight, age 12
WHAT Stop-motion safety device
WHEN 1850
WHERE New Hampshire

Margaret Knight's brothers worked in a cotton textile mill. One day, their younger sister paid them a visit, and while there, she witnessed a serious accident. A heavy machine malfunctioned and injured a worker. Knight went home and started tinkering. She invented a device that would automatically shut down a machine whenever a malfunction occurred. Knight went on to create many more inventions, including her most famous—a machine that folds and glues paper into bags with flat bottoms that's still in use today.

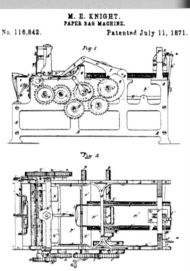

WHO Louis Braille, age 15
WHAT Braille
WHEN 1924
WHERE Paris, France

When he was three years old, Louis Braille became blind as a result of an infection. Braille went to school and memorized everything his teachers said. When he was 10, he entered a special school for the blind. Two years later, he heard a lecture about sonography, a method of reading and writing raised symbols that soldiers used so they could communicate at night.

When Braille was 15, he began fiddling with the "night writing," until he had a six-dot code. At age 20, he published an account that explained his code and how it worked. Braille's alphabet is now used in nearly every country in the world.

WHO George Nissen, age 16
WHAT Trampoline
WHEN 1926 to 1934
WHERE Cedar Rapids, Iowa

The circus had come to town, and George Nissen was staring at the trapeze artists as they glided through the air. As a gymnast on his high school's team, he must have watched in awe. He also noticed the netting that allowed the trapeze artists to bounce onto the swinging bars and caught them if they fell.

Nissen went home and started tinkering in his parents' garage. Before long, he devised a steel frame that he'd stretched with canvas. That early model was the beginning of what would become Nissen's great invention: the trampoline.

WHO Chester Greenwood, age 15
WHAT Earmuffs
WHEN 1873
WHERE Farmington, Maine

Except for the cold, Chester Greenwood enjoyed ice skating. Testing a new pair of skates on one especially freezing day, he couldn't keep his ears warm. Allergic to wool, he couldn't wear the scarves most kids used.

Frustrated, Greenwood took some wire and twisted it into two ovals. Then he asked his grandmother to sew fur onto them. That did the trick. Later, Greenwood fine-tuned his model and added a steel band to hold the muffs in place. He patented his invention, calling it the Greenwood's Champion Ear Protector. Today, we know them as earmuffs.

WHAT Are Some Foods Invented by Accident?

Many discoveries come about by accident or by an out-and-out mistake. When that happens with food inventions, the results are often lip-smackingly good.

WHAT Chocolate Chip Cookies
WHO Ruth Wakefield, innkeeper
WHEN 1930
WHERE Toll House Inn, Whitman, Massachusetts

One day, Ruth Wakefield ran out of baking chocolate while preparing a batch of cookies for her guests. All she had on hand was a chocolate candy bar, so she broke it up and added the pieces to her batter. She expected the chocolate to melt evenly. Instead, the cookies were studded with gooey bits of chocolate, and a new treat was born.

WHAT Cereal Flakes
WHO John Harvey Kellogg and Will Keith Kellogg
WHEN 1894
WHERE Battle Creek, Michigan

Waste not; want not. That's what the Kellogg brothers, who ran a home for people in poor health, believed. So when Will left some boiled wheat sitting out and it went stale, the two men attempted to turn it into long sheets of dough. Instead, the wheat came out of the rollers in flakes, which the brothers toasted and served to their patients. The cereal was a hit. Later, the brothers tried their new technique on other grains, including corn.

WHAT Potato Chips
WHO George Crum
WHEN 1853
WHERE Moon Lake House,
Saratoga Springs, New York

Customers can be tough to please. Chef George Crum knew that all too well. A guest at his inn kept returning his fried potatoes, claiming they weren't crisp enough. The chef had enough. He sliced a new batch of potatoes as thin as he could, fried them in oil, and sprinkled salt on them. The dish wasn't returned and soon other guests wanted their potatoes made the same way.

WHAT Ice-Cream Cones
WHO Ernest Hamwi
WHEN 1904
WHERE World's Fair, St. Louis, Missouri

Arnold Fornachou, a vendor at the fair, had just run out of paper dishes to serve his ice cream, and customers were lining up. He turned to his fellow vendors for help. Ernest Hamwi came to the rescue. He rolled up his waffle-like pastries and gave them to Fornachou to fill with ice cream. Later, Hamwi received a patent for a pastry cone-making machine and started his own company.

WHAT Is a Dirigible?

Any aircraft that's filled with a lighter-than-air gas and can be steered is a dirigible. Instead of wings like an airplane, a dirigible uses rudders and propellers to navigate through the air. There are two basic kinds of dirigibles. One is the rigid airship, which has a rigid frame, or skeleton, underneath its covering. The second kind is the blimp, which doesn't have a rigid frame. Both types are typically filled with helium—a gas that enables the dirigibles to fly.

A blimp doesn't have a rigid frame, so it deflates like a balloon when its helium is removed.

Henri Giffard flew the first prototype of the dirigible in the 1850s. By the early 1900s, they were popular across the world. Today, dirigibles are mostly used for advertising and sightseeing purposes. If you go to pro-football games, you may have seen a blimp providing overhead coverage of the game.

The *Hindenburg* Disaster

The *Hindenburg*, a luxury airship built by Zeppelin, a German company, was the largest airship in the world. More than 800 feet long, it needed more than seven million cubic feet of hydrogen to fill it. On May 3, 1937, it took off from Frankfurt, Germany. Aboard were 61 crew members and 36 passengers. Three days later, it attempted to land at Lakehurst, New Jersey, in poor weather conditions. Suddenly the airship caught fire and was consumed in flames. Remarkably, 62 of the people on board survived. To this day, no one knows for sure what started the fire, but because the airship used flammable hydrogen instead of the safer helium, it burned in minutes.

WHAT Is Kevlar?

Plenty of police officers and soldiers owe their lives to Kevlar, the main material used in bullet-proof vests. Considered a miracle fiber, Kevlar has five times the strength of steel yet is lightweight and flexible. Another big plus is that it doesn't rust, corrode, or tear. That makes it an ideal material to use in underwater cables, boat hulls, and pieces of spacecraft.

A New Spin on Fiber

So how did such a super-strong fiber come about? In 1964, Stephanie Kwolek was working as a researcher for DuPont, an American chemical company. Her team was asked to develop high-performance fibers that were strong, lightweight, and that didn't melt at high temperatures.

One day she melted a polymer—a substance that nylon, rubber, and vinyl are made of—into a liquid. Kwolek took the solution to be spun in a spinneret, a machine that turns liquid polymers into fiber. The fiber that came out was tested to see how strong it was. The results were amazing. The fiber was both strong and lightweight. Today, Kevlar is used to make safety helmets, firefighters' suits, radial tires, suspension bridge cables, brake pads, and racing sails.

WHAT'S More . . .

Ounce for ounce, Kevlar is stronger than steel, but spider silk is even stronger. And toughest of all is the silk from the Darwin's bark spider, an arachnid that lives in the jungles of Madagascar. The orb webs from these spiders are enormous, and can span rivers, streams, and lakes.

WHAT Is a Boomerang?

The boomerang is a curved missile that spins through the air and may return to the thrower. Boomerangs have been around for a very long time. One discovered in Poland, was carved from a mammoth's tusk and is about 30,000 years old. Experts say it was a non-returning boomerang—it didn't come back after it was thrown. They think it was used as a weapon to hunt animals. Returning boomerangs were first used in Australia about 10,000 years ago. There, the native people, called Aborigines, developed a returning boomerang for fun and sport. And that's the role they still play today.

Modern boomerangs can be shaped like a banana, an *X*, or a question mark. Today's versions are made from a variety of materials, including plywood, plastic, aluminum, and fiberglass.

WHAT'S More...

Boomerang fans test their skills at tournaments. They compete at different events, such as long distance, doubling (throwing two boomerangs at the same time), and fast catch (the most catches in five minutes).

A player competes in a boomerang championship in Delaware.

A Really BIG Boomerang

At almost nine feet from tip to tip and weighing 2.3 pounds, the world's largest returning boomerang is not easy to throw. The boomerang has a handle where its two wings meet. The thrower holds the handle and hoists the boomerang on his back before launching it forward. It can fly about 75 feet.

Make Your Own Boomerang

What You Need

- cardboard from the back of an old cereal box
- ruler
- pencil
- scissors
- stapler

What to Do

1. Measure and cut out two 8-inch-by-¾-inch rectangles from the cardboard.

2. Place one rectangle over the other so that the two pieces are perpendicular to each other. Staple through the center where they cross. You should now have an X-shaped object with four arms.

3. Cut ⅛ inch off the side of each arm as shown.

4. Round each arm's tip.

5. To throw your boomerang, go outdoors. Holding one of the arms vertically at its tip, bring the boomerang so that it is just past your ear.

6. Then move your forearm forward, flicking your wrist as you do so and releasing the boomerang. If you don't get your boomerang to return on the first try, keep practicing until you get the hang of it.

WHAT Is a Geodesic Dome?

A geodesic dome is hard to miss. The structure is shaped like a partial sphere, and it's made up of interlocking pyramid shapes called tetrahedrons. Lightweight, yet extremely strong and stable, the geodesic dome uses less material to cover more space than any other structure ever built.

A Man Ahead of His Time

The man who patented the geodesic dome was Buckminster Fuller, an American engineer and inventor. In the 1950s, he designed the geodesic dome in an effort to provide low-cost housing. While the domes never caught on as places to live, they are used as airplane hangars, greenhouses, observatories, theaters, sports arenas, and planetariums.

Buckminster Fuller stands in front of one of his geodesic domes.

WHAT'S More...

Before Fuller's invention, domes needed to be supported with vaults or flying buttresses.

flying buttress

vault

Famous Geodesic Domes

Designed by Buckminster Fuller for Expo 67, the 1967 world's fair in Montreal, Canada, the Biosphere is now a museum dedicated to the environment.

A complete sphere, Spaceship Earth is more a globe than a dome. Still, the Disney World attraction is perhaps the most famous geodesic dome ever built. It towers 180 feet high and can easily be seen for miles around.

WHAT Is a Hovercraft?

Imagine a vehicle that can travel on water, land, or ice. Does that make it a plane, a car, or a boat? It's the hovercraft, a vehicle that glides over land or sea on a cushion of air powered by air propellers or jet engines.

High-pressurized vents of air supplied by a powered fan underneath the craft press down on the surface, lifting the vehicle slightly. This constant air source is trapped by the vehicle's skirt, reducing friction and allowing it to move forward smoothly.

A Crafty Inventor

Christopher Cockerell, an English inventor, wanted to make the boat he was building go faster. He figured that a vehicle suspended on a cushion of air would quickly skim the water's surface. However, any fan he used would be larger than the boat. After trial and error, Cockerell realized that pressurized air around the rim of the boat could cause it to rise.

Out of Luck, Then Success

In 1952, Cockerell got busy designing and testing a model. He took it to the British government, thinking the armed forces could benefit from his invention. Although his idea was classified top secret, Cockerell didn't receive any money to develop the hovercraft further. He later complained, "The Navy said it was a plane not a boat; the Air Force said it was a boat not a plane; and the Army were 'plain not interested.'"

The SR-N1

Five years later, the inventor built a full-scale model, the SR-N1. On July 25, 1959, the SR-N1 successfully crossed the English Channel in a little over two hours.

WHAT'S More...

Large hovercraft glide along at an average of 35 mph, while lighter craft can go as fast as 70 mph. The world record is 85 mph, set by Bob Windt in 1995.

What Are They Good For?

Hovercraft transport people, equipment, and other vehicles across all kinds of terrain.

○ Hovercraft fly over shallow water, thin ice, rapids, swamps, and even deserts to rescue people in danger.

○ The military uses hovercraft to transport tanks and other heavy equipment.

○ Oil companies use flat-deck hovercraft to transport equipment across mud flats.

This hovercraft is about to come ashore on the Isle of Wight.

WHAT Is Zorbing?

If you've ever seen a hamster running inside a clear ball, you have some idea of what zorbing is all about. Only you're the hamster. In this extreme sport, you ride inside a large plastic ball down a slope.

A zorb consists of two balls, a smaller one inside a larger one, connected by ropes to keep the balls turning as a unit. The air cushion that forms between the balls protects the rider from bumps. Both balls are made of see-through plastic. So how do you get in—and out of—a zorb? There's a two-foot-long opening for a rider to squeeze through.

Zorbing was invented by two New Zealanders in the early 1990s. Andrew Akers and Dwayne van der Sluis wanted to create a device that would make it possible for them to walk on water. The two friends ended up with a prototype of a ball within a ball. The finished product did float, but it was impossible to steer.

Even so, the men still thought they had a great idea and decided to patent and trademark their invention. They called it the zorb. Before long, the partners hit on the bizarre idea of strapping people inside the zorb and rolling them down hills.

Are You a Dry or Wet Zorber?

There are two types of zorbing rides to choose from. For a dry ride, an operator straps you into the ball, and after making sure you're secure, releases the zorb. Down the slope you roll, head over heels, until you reach the bottom. There, another operator stops the zorb and unstraps you.

If you decide on a wet ride, you aren't strapped in. Instead the operator fills the zorb with about five gallons of water and off you go. People have compared the experience to being inside a washing machine.

WHAT Will Future Transportation Be Like?

Cars

Many transportation innovations of the future already exist. The challenge is how to make these energy-saving vehicles work more efficiently so they can replace the fossil-fuel vehicles we ride in today. For instance, electric vehicles that run on batteries need to be improved so they can travel longer distances. Today, most electric cars can run for about 100 miles before its battery has to be recharged.

Engineers are developing an electric two-wheeled vehicle called P.U.M.A. (Personal Urban Mobility and Accessibility). Running on a lithium battery, the small, space-saving, 300-pound vehicle would ease city traffic jams.

What will the future hold? Will we go to work in flying cars? Vacation on the moon? Snarf down meat grown in test tubes? Here are some expert predictions.

Trains

Today, commuters in some big cities in China and Japan ride on high-speed maglev trains. (Maglev stands for magnetic levitation.) Such a train doesn't need wheels. Instead, it uses magnets to raise—or levitate—the train inches above the track. Futurists—people who think about the future and how we will live—believe maglevs will replace traditional trains in the U.S and around the world.

A maglev can travel at speeds of more than 300 mph, offering smooth, quiet rides.

Planes

Other solutions for future transportation exist only as ideas. Personal flying vehicles are an exciting possibility. A NASA engineer designed the Puffin, a one-person, electric, flying craft. Right now the Puffin is just a concept, but one day you might zip around in one.

To fly the Puffin, the pilot lies flat on his or her stomach. When not in use, the vehicle would rest on its tail.

WHAT Will Space Travel Be Like?

Sixty years ago, space travel existed only in science-fiction novels. Today, astronauts have landed on the moon and lived in space for more than a year. What will the future hold for travel to the farthest reaches of our solar system?

Solar Sail

A spacecraft's weight is about 95% rocket fuel, making long-distance space flight extremely expensive. But what if there were a way to reduce the amount of fuel by harnessing the sun's energy to propel spacecraft once they reach space? Engineers are experimenting with solar-sail powered craft. Such a craft, made of lightweight, reflective material, would use sunlight as its power. Light particles bouncing off the reflective sail would push the craft forward at a faster and faster speed. A solar sail, however, would not be able to reach space on its own. It would need a traditional rocket to launch it. Once in space, though, the sail would have endless power from the sun and could travel indefinitely.

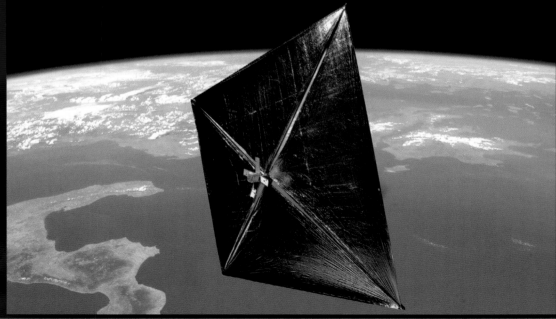

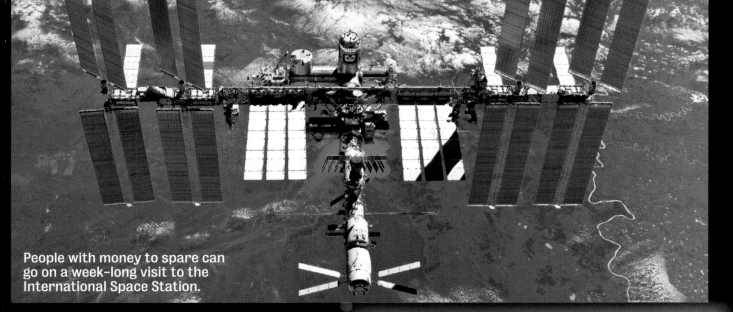

People with money to spare can go on a week-long visit to the International Space Station.

Space Tourism

Do you have $20 million to spare? That's the current price for a one-week stay at the International Space Station. So far, at least five people have paid to experience life in space. Like astronauts, the tourists must prepare for their trip, spending several months training. In the years to come, more and more people will visit space. There is even talk of developing space hotels, where tourists could vacation and take spacewalks.

Elevator to the Stars

Engineers are developing an elevator to send people into space without rockets! The space elevator would let a spacecraft climb a cable into the sky. Made of a paper-thin yet incredibly strong and flexible material, a ribbon-shaped cable would reach more than 60,000 miles into space where it would end at a platform. The bottom of the cable would be anchored in the ocean. People and cargo would ride up the elevator on mechanical lifters. Once at the top, they would board a traditional spacecraft and zoom off to their final destination.

Platform

Cable

Lifter

Anchor in ocean

EARTH

WHAT Will We Be Eating for Dinner?

In the next 50 years, another two to three billion people will be living—and eating—on Earth. With so many mouths to feed, scientists are looking for ways to guarantee there will be enough food to go around. This may include developing super crops that resist disease, insects, and weather extremes, so that they yield bigger harvests. Eating readily available sources of protein, such as insects and algae, simple, one-celled plants, is another suggestion.

But probably the most unusual idea of what will be on our table years from now is meat grown in laboratories. Why would scientists want to do that? Raising livestock takes up a lot of land. The animals consume huge amounts of plants and put out greenhouse gases that are bad for the environment.

When cows belch and pass gas, they give off methane, a greenhouse gas that traps heat in the atmosphere and has been linked to global warming. One adult cow can produce up to 400 pounds a year. Worldwide, cows and other cud-chewing animals produce 80 million metric tons of the gas.

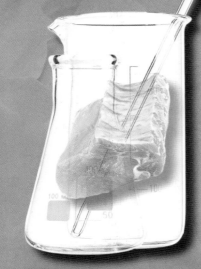

The first meat successfully grown in a lab came from goldfish cells. NASA conducted the experiments in 2000, hoping to provide astronauts on long space trips with fresh meat. Nine years later, Dutch scientists produced pork from the cells of a pig.

Although it is technically possible to make test-tube meat, scientists are not able to produce it in large amounts. Plus it takes about one million dollars to produce eight ounces of test-tube beef. (That's one pricey steak!) Until scientists figure out how to make it cheaper and quicker, test-tube meat will only be food for thought.

Dirt-Free Salad

Carrots, radishes, and lettuce grown without soil? In the future, that might be how most vegetables are raised. It's all thanks to hydroponics—a way to grow crops in water without a speck of soil. As Earth's population skyrockets and farming land declines, hydroponics will provide farmers with another choice. Crops can thrive in underground vaults, on rooftops, greenhouses, and in buildings designed for this space-saving farming method.

WHAT Animals May Become Extinct?

More than 230 million years ago, dinosaurs walked the planet. About 165 million years later, they were extinct, most likely done in by a massive asteroid that crashed into Earth.

In the not-so-distant future, many species of animals that are alive today may follow in the dinosaurs' footsteps. Most will have been done in not by an object from space, but because of humans. As people chop down more and more forests, take over vast amounts of land for crops, and pollute the air and oceans, animals are disappearing at a frightening rate.

Top 10 Endangered Species

Leatherback turtle

Sumatran orangutan

Mountain gorilla

Atlantic bluefin tuna

Vaquita

Source: World Wildlife Fund

Tiger

Snow leopard

Irrawaddy dolphin

Javan rhino

Asian elephant

Your Help Matters

The good news is that conservation efforts have helped save many animals from becoming extinct. In the 1960s, the bald eagle was in danger of being wiped out, with fewer than 450 nesting pairs in the continental U.S. Today, there are close to 10,000 couples and the future looks bright.

Here are some ways you can help save threatened animals:

○ Learn all you can about endangered animals. The more you know, the more you can help.

○ Share what you learn with others. Pick an endangered animal and do a school project on it, or design a poster and put it up where people can see it.

○ Write and put on a play about an endangered animal. Cast your friends and perform it at school or at a community center.

○ Hold a fundraiser for endangered animals. You and your friends and neighbors can raise money by holding a bake sale, a car wash, or a yard sale.

○ Adopt an endangered animal. Many organizations allow you to "adopt" an animal. The World Wildlife Fund is a good place to start.

○ Volunteer at a nature center or wildlife refuge that cares for endangered animals.

○ Write a letter to your senators or local representatives and tell them why it is important to protect endangered species. Encourage your friends and neighbors to write, too.

WHAT Was the Roanoke Colony?

In 1580, John White strode through the dense woods of what is now an island off the coast of North Carolina. He was headed toward the Roanoke fort, home to England's first settlement in the New World. White was governor of the small colony, and he was returning after a three-year absence.

The Mysterious Word

When he reached the fort, White was met with silence. None of the 117 colonists were there to greet him. Even the houses inside the fort had vanished. Only the posts that made up the stockade remained.

White read a word carved on one of the posts: CROATOAN. He stared at the carving in disbelief. What had happened to the colony? What had happened to his family? And what exactly, did CROATOAN mean?

White never discovered the colony's fate. The governor searched for the missing settlers and then returned to England.

In the more than 400 years since the mysterious disappearance of the Roanoke colony, historians continue to wonder what became of it. That has led to a number of theories about what might have happened.

John White depicted an Indian settlement in this drawing.

Not every event in history can be explained. From hidden treasures to famous disappearances to, these history mysteries are waiting to be solved.

Why Did the Colony Disappear?

Going Native

The word CROATOAN is an important clue. The Croatoan Indians were a nearby tribe that got along well with the colonists. Did the colonists leave the fort to live near or among the Indians? If the settlers were short of food and supplies, this would have made sense. But if the English did go off to live with the Croatoans, they should still be alive—and there was no trace of them.

In Enemy Hands

Perhaps a hostile Indian tribe killed the colonists. Several tribes lived in the Roanoke area and not all were friendly with the settlers. If the colony packed up and moved inland, they may have met up with one of these tribes and been captured or killed.

Starved to Death

Another idea is that the colonists died from hunger or disease. While this is a possibility, it's unlikely that every single settler would have died under these circumstances. Also, John White didn't find any gravesites at the abandoned fort.

The 1896 Memorial Marker at Fort Raleigh National Historic Site

Archaeologists look for clues about the lost colony.

WHAT Is the Mystery Behind Amelia Earhart's Disappearance?

Amelia Earhart was a pioneer in the sky. In 1928, she became the first woman passenger to cross the Atlantic Ocean in a plane. She was also the first female to fly solo across the U.S. without stopping. But as the world-famous pilot told reporters, "I think I have just one more long flight in my system."

So on June 1, 1937, Earhart set off from Miami, Florida, with her navigator, Fred Noonan. She was beginning her most incredible trip yet. The two were headed around the world! For the next month the pair flew to South America, and then on to Africa, Asia, and Australia. By the time the plane reached Papua New Guinea, an island north of Australia, the two had flown 22,000 miles. The next leg of their journey was the riskiest. The flyers had to head for tiny Howland Island, a speck in the vast Pacific Ocean, and more than 2,500 miles away.

On the morning of July 2, Earhart and Noonan took off for Howland Island, on what they thought would be an 18-hour flight. The plane had barely enough fuel to reach the island.

Bad Weather

As they drew nearer to Howland, the plane hit bad weather. Thick clouds and rain made it hard to navigate. Earhart and a Coast Guard radio crew were able to communicate for a while. They heard Earhart report that the weather was bad and the plane's fuel was running low. She ended her final message with the words, "We are running north and south." She was never heard from again. She and Fred Noonan vanished somewhere in the Pacific.

A huge search for the pilot and her navigator began almost at once. But no sign of Earhart, Noonan, or wreckage of the plane was ever found.

What Happened?

In 1940, some people working on an island not far from Howland, discovered a human skull, some bones, soles from both a man and a woman's shoe, and a box used to hold navigating equipment. Did Earhart and Noonan reach this deserted island and set up camp? The evidence vanished over the years, and Earhart's disappearance continues to be an unsolved history mystery. But the pilot will always be remembered for her courage and for her pioneering role in the history of flight.

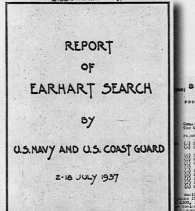

Pages from the U.S. Navy report on the search for Earhart

The red line shows the route that Earhart flew until her plane disappeared.

WHAT Is the Oak Island Treasure Mystery?

What is buried in the Money Pit on Oak Island, Nova Scotia? The mystery has baffled treasure seekers ever since the pit was first discovered in 1795. That's when a teenage boy hunting on the uninhabited tiny island along Canada's Atlantic coast, came upon a wide depression hidden with tree branches. He'd heard tales of pirates burying treasure in the area, so he came back with two friends and they began digging. Every 10 feet down, the boys uncovered a platform of wooden logs. The hole was some sort of a shaft that had been refilled with dirt. The trio reached 30 feet down and, with no treasure in sight, had to stop.

But they didn't give up. Nine years later, they convinced a wealthy businessman to form a company to hunt for the treasure. This time they got down past 90 feet. Again, they found wooden platforms every 10 feet, as well as coconut matting and a stone carved with some kind of code. They were definitely on to something! At 93 feet, they struck something solid. Was it the treasure chest at last? They didn't find out. The next morning, the pit was two-thirds filled with water. Unable to bail out the water, the men gave up digging.

CANADA

Oak Island

Water Traps

In 1849, another group started digging for the treasure. But the drillers had the same problems with water filling the hole. The crew figured out that the people who built the pit had installed a system of flood tunnels. Each was a trap designed to fill the hole with water to prevent the treasure from ever being found.

Today, the island is owned by businessmen hoping to finally unearth the treasure—if there is any. Will they succeed and if so, what will they find? Stay tuned.

Many treasure hunters, including President Franklin D. Roosevelt, have tried to find treasure at Oak Island, Nova Scotia.

WHAT'S More...

O The only treasure ever found at the site were three links of a gold chain, dug up in 1849.

O Some people believe the Money Pit is actually a sinkhole—a depression in the ground caused by water erosion.

WHAT Is the Mystery Behind Winchester House?

Staircases that lead nowhere, windows that look into other parts of the house, columns built upside-down. Those are just a few of the odd features visitors find when they tour the mysterious Winchester House in San Jose, California. Building started in 1884 and continued—uninterrupted—for the next 38 years. The construction ended only when the mansion's owner, Sarah Winchester, died. By that time, the mansion had 160 rooms, 361 steps, and 10,000 windowpanes.

Sarah was the widow of William Wirt Winchester, a wealthy rifle manufacturer. After her husband died in 1881, Sarah, who was very sad, visited a medium, someone who claimed to speak to the dead. The medium told Sarah she was haunted by the spirits of people killed by her husband's rifles. She wouldn't find peace unless Winchester built a home for herself but not complete it. According to the medium, an ever-changing house would confuse the ghosts. Sarah believed every word.

Today, Winchester House is on the National Register of Historic Places. If you are ever in San Jose, you can visit it and see it for yourself. Tour guides advise that you don't wander off. If you do, you might be lost for hours in the twisty maze of the building.

WHAT Were the Cottingley Fairies?

Do fairies really exist? According to Elsie Wright and her cousin Frances Griffiths, they do. And the two even took photos to prove it. In 1917, the girls claimed they saw fairies in the garden of Elsie's home in the English village of Cottingley. Elsie borrowed her father's camera and took a photograph of Frances with several of the spirits. A month later, Frances took a photo of Elsie shaking hands with a gnome.

The photos might have been forgotten, if Elsie's mother hadn't decided to show them to a man who believed the dead could talk to the living. He showed them to several people, including a photography expert who declared the pictures were genuine.

The Mystery Gets Solved

News of the photos spread. Then a famous writer asked the girls to take more pictures until there were a total of five.

Eventually the photos and the fairies were forgotten. It wasn't until the 1980s that Elsie admitted that she and her cousin had faked the pictures. She had drawn cutout figures of the fairies based on drawings from a children's book. Frances agreed that the first four photos were a hoax, but said that the fifth photo was real. Both women insisted that they had seen real live fairies.

Elsie shakes hands with a gnome.

Frances and the spirits. Real or fake?

WHAT Is Spelunking?

Some people put on snorkeling equipment and swim around ocean reefs. Other people suit up and climb to the tops of mountains. But spelunkers slap on helmets and venture deep into the Earth. Spelunking is the exploration of underground caves.

Why would people plunge thousands of feet underground into a world of strange shapes and total darkness? According to author James Tabor who wrote a book about caving, it's the challenge.

"There are some people who, when they look at a high mountain or a deep ocean or a bizarre cave, something really deep, deep, deep in them says, 'I've got to go there.' It's almost an irresistible impulse," Tabor explains.

An Awesome Journey

Spelunkers face dangers including the possibility of drowning in underground lakes and rivers, being hit with poison gases, or being buried under rockfalls. That's one reason why spelunkers explore in groups. For them the payoff is well worth the risk. Coming across strange and colorful rock formations, going where no one else has gone before, and spotting cave-dwelling creatures make the experience an under-this-world adventure.

WHAT'S More . . .

Many people call their sport caving and prefer to be known as cavers. In the United Kingdom, the sport is called potholing.

Light from aboveground shines through cracks in the Earth, providing light for spelunkers.

A spelunker travels through a cave.

Some spelunkers swim in underwater caves.

Glossary

algae primitive plants that have no roots, stems, or leaves, and live mainly in water

arachnid an arthropod having four pairs of legs, such as spiders and scorpions

archaeologist a scientist who studies how people in the past lived using information gained from artifacts of that culture, such as pottery and tools

asteroid rocks, some the size of small planets, that orbit between Mars and Jupiter

atmosphere the envelope of gases around the Earth

cells the basic structure of all living things

dirigible an aircraft that can be steered or guided

endangered a species, or type of living thing, that is in immediate danger of becoming extinct, or dying out completely

flying buttress a support built against a wall and forming an arch

fossil fuels fuels, such as oil and coal, that are created by plant and animal matter over millions of years

global warming an increase in the average temperature of the Earth

GPS (Global Positioning System) a satellite navigation system that is used to determine an exact location on Earth

gravity the force of attraction between two objects

greenhouse gas a gas, such as carbon dioxide or methane, that helps cause global warming

hieroglyphic a type of writing, such as one used by ancient Egyptians, that uses picture symbols to represent words or sounds

hydroponics a method of growing plants in nutrient solutions rather than soil

Madagascar an island off the southeastern coast of Africa

orbit the path one body takes around another, such as the path of the Earth around the sun

pollution the contamination of air, water, or soil by harmful substances

polymer a natural or synthetic compound that is made up of repeated links of simple molecules

protein a substance basic to living cells and necessary for an organism to function; it is an important source of energy in a person's diet

satellite a natural or manmade object that revolves around a planet

species a group of similar organisms

spinneret a machine that turns liquid polymers into fiber

stockade a defensive barrier made of stakes or timber

tetrahedron a solid figure formed by four triangular faces

tornado a dark, funnel-shaped cloud made of fast-spinning air

tusk a long, constantly growing front tooth that appears, usually in pairs, in certain animals, such as elephants

Index